What Is A Machine

By B. John Syrocki, Ed. D.

Professor of Science
State University of New York

Pictures — Gregory Orloff

BENEFIC PRESS • CHICAGO
PUBLISHING DIVISION OF BECKLEY-CARDY COMPANY

The WHAT IS IT Series

What Is A Bird
What Is A Cow
What Is A Fish
What Is A Frog
What Is A Plant
What Is A Tree

What Is Air
What Is Light
What Is Heat
What Is A Cell
What Is Water
What Is Sound
What Is Space
What Is A Star
What Is A Bee
What Is Soil
What Is Gravity
What Is A Rock
What Is Energy
What Is A Reptile

What Is A Season
What Is A Turtle
What Is A Chicken
What Is The Earth
What Is A Butterfly
What Is A Simple Machine

What Is Matter
What Is A Magnet
What Is A Rocket
What Is A Rodent
What Is A Solar System
What Is A Human
What Is A Machine
What Is Chemistry
What Is Weather
What Is Electricity
What Is An Atom
What Is An Insect
What Is A Dinosaur
What Is Electronic Communication

Library of Congress
Number 60-6587

CONTENTS

THIS IS A MACHINE

A machine is something made by man
to do work for him.

Machines can make man's work easier. They can do
work faster than man. Sometimes machines can do
work that man cannot do at all.

This machine washes clothes for us.

This machine takes us up and down stairs.

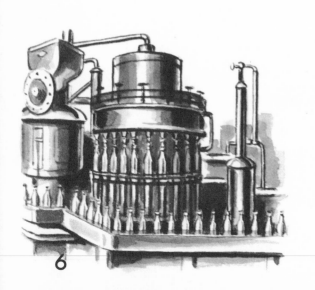

This machine puts caps on bottles faster than a man can do it.

No man could lift such large, heavy girders. But it is easy work for this big machine.

This machine can help man to add numbers.

There is even a machine to make doughnuts.

We often speak of six simple machines which help us in certain ways. Many big machines are made by using one or more forms of these six simple machines.

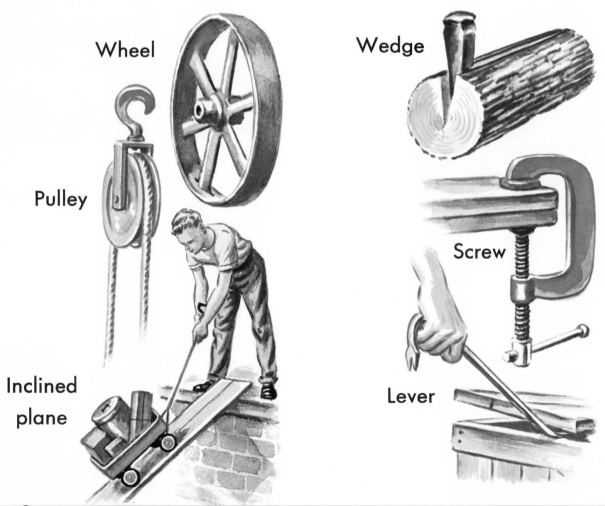

Wheel

Wedge

Pulley

Screw

Inclined plane

Lever

THE WHEEL

A ball rolls on all of
its curved surface. It
can roll in any direction.

If we cut a piece from the center of the ball, the
piece rolls only on its curved side. The piece can roll
in only two directions, backward or forward. The
piece is a wheel.

Wheels are made from different kinds of materials. They may be made from wood, metal, rubber, and many other materials.

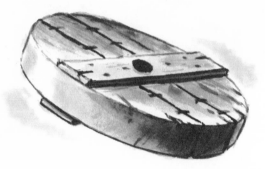

This wheel is solid wood.

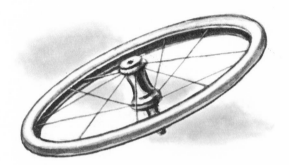

This wheel has spokes.

Some wheels have teeth.

There are thick wheels and thin wheels.

A wheel is often put on a round bar called an axle.

A hole is made in the center of the wheel. The axle is placed through the hole in the wheel.

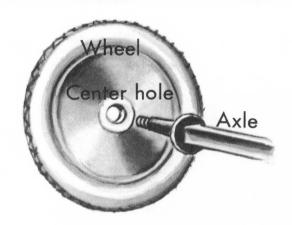

The wheel spins around the axle.

Wheels and axles make it easy for us to move heavy things.

This box is flat on the ground. It takes five children to move it.

If the box is put on wheels and axles, it takes only one child to move the same box.

The box on wheels is easier to move than the box flat on the ground because there is less friction. When the children try to move the box without wheels, the ground rubs against the entire bottom of the box.

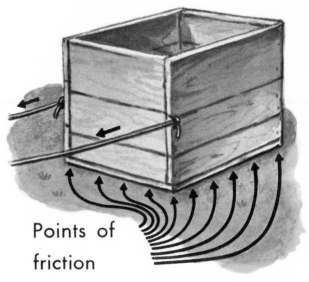

Points of friction

This rubbing or friction tends to stop the box from moving.

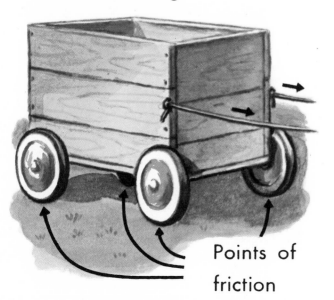

Points of friction

But if the box is on wheels, there is friction on only a small part of the wheels. The wheels will roll instead of sliding over the ground. This makes less friction, and less force is needed to move the box.

Sometimes two wheels
are connected by a belt.
The two wheels on this
lawn mower are connected
by a belt. As one wheel
turns, the belt turns the other
wheel. The power from the
motor passes from one
wheel to another.

A chain is often used to connect two wheels. The large pedal wheel on a bicycle is connected with the small back wheel by a chain.

Both wheels have teeth to hold the chain. Toothed wheels are called gears.

The rider pushes on the pedals to turn the large gear. The connecting chain makes the small gear turn in the same direction. The force of the pedaling passes from one gear to the other.

A large wheel can be used to make a smaller wheel turn faster.

The large gear on a bicycle is three times the size of the small gear. The large gear makes one complete turn while the small one makes three.

The small gear turns faster because it makes more complete turns than the large one in the same amount of time.

Sometimes a small wheel is used to make a larger wheel turn more slowly.

The small wheel here is connected by a belt with a wheel twice as big. A motor turns the small wheel, and the belt makes the large wheel turn.

But the large wheel turns more slowly than the small wheel. The small wheel turns two times for every time the large wheel turns once.

We have read about gears connected by a chain. Sometimes gears are placed so that the teeth of one fit between the teeth of the other. The gears in automobiles are placed in this way.

We can tell how fast or how slowly one gear will turn another by counting the number of teeth on each one.

This large gear has 40 teeth. The small one has only 10. The small gear turns four times faster than the large gear.

The large gear here has sixty teeth. The small one has ten. The large gear turns the small gear six times as fast because it has six times as many teeth.

A motor or some other force must turn the first gear. The second gear passes the force along to another point. A rod is often used to receive the force from the second gear. The power is passed along this way in an automobile.

This small gear has ten teeth. The large gear has twenty. The small gear turns the large gear half as fast as the small gear turns because it has half as many teeth.

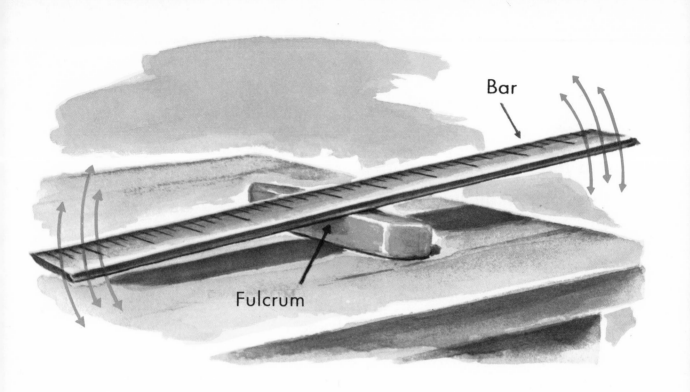

Bar

Fulcrum

THE LEVER

A lever is a bar or plank used to move things.

A lever may be made of metal, wood, or any other material that is hard and strong.

For a lever to work, it must rest on a steady object and be free to move in different directions. This steady object is called the fulcrum.

The things or thing to be moved by the lever is called the load.

The push or pull which moves the lever is called the force.

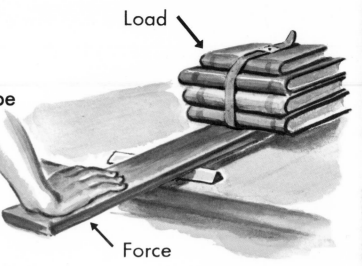

Load

Force

The side of the lever the load is on is the load arm.

The other side is the force arm.

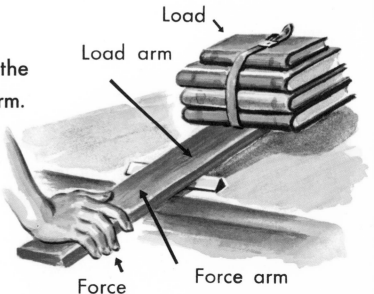

Load

Load arm

Force arm

Force

Levers are divided into three different classes. The position of the load, the force, and the fulcrum is different for each class.

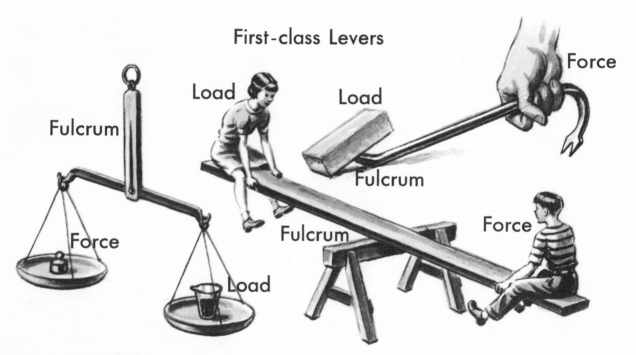

First-class Levers

Fulcrum

Load

Load

Force

Force

Fulcrum

Fulcrum

Force

Load

The three levers in the picture are all first-class levers. The fulcrum is always between the load and the force in levers of this class.

The lever is useful because it can make it possible for a man to lift a heavy load without pushing very hard on the force arm.

Let us see how a first-class lever can help this boy to lift a rock which weighs 60 pounds.

60 inches

60 pounds

The boy has a strong metal rod which is 60 inches long. He also has a small log for a fulcrum.

First, he places the fulcrum at the center of the rod. He places the end of the rod under the rock. The load arm is exactly the same length as the force arm.

When the force arm and the load arm are of equal lengths, the boy must push with 60 pounds of force in order to lift the 60-pound rock.

60 pounds of force

60 pounds

30 inches

Fulcrum

30 inches

But the boy is not strong
enough to push down with
60 pounds of force. So he
moves the fulcrum closer
to the load.

Now the load arm is 1/2
as long as the force arm.
1/2 of 40=20

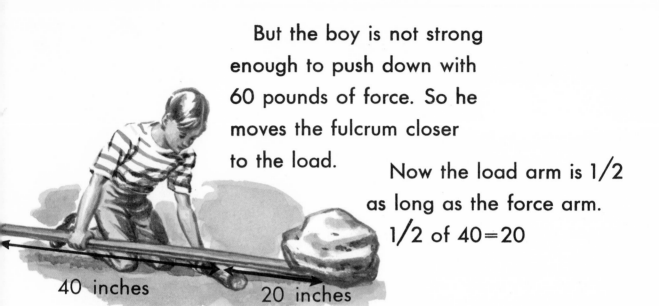

40 inches   20 inches

The boy needs to push down with a force that is
only 1/2 the weight of the load.
1/2 of 60=30
The boy pushes down with 30 pounds of force.
He lifts the rock easily.

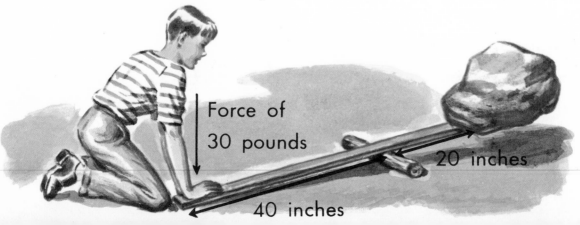

Force of
30 pounds

20 inches

40 inches

The girl is not strong enough to push with even 30 pounds of force. She moves the fulcrum still closer to the load. Now the load arm is only 1/4 as long as the force arm.

1/4 of 48=12

The girl needs to push down with a force equal to 1/4 the load.

1/4 of 60=15

When the girl pushes with 15 pounds of force, she can easily lift the rock.

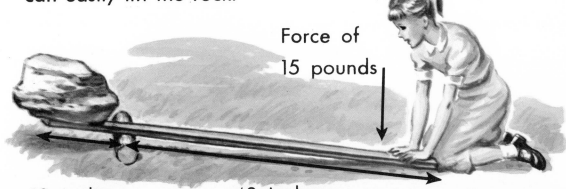

Force of
15 pounds

12 inches   48 inches

When speaking of levers of the first class, we often say that the force is multiplied or made greater as it travels along the lever from the force to the load. The force is multiplied by the number of load arms needed to equal the length of one force arm.

The boy's push of 30 pounds was multiplied by 2. It would take 2 load arms to equal the length of the force arm.

By the time the boy's push reached the load, it was equal to 60 pounds. It lifted the rock.

$$
\begin{array}{r}
30 \\
\times 2 \\
\hline
60
\end{array}
$$

30 — Boy's push

×2 — Number of load arms needed to equal length of one force arm

60 — Weight of the load

The girl's push of 15 pounds was multiplied by 4. It would take 4 load arms to equal the length of the force arm.

$$
\begin{array}{r}
15 \\
\times 4 \\
\hline
60
\end{array}
$$

15 — Girl's push

×4 — Number of load arms needed to equal length of one force arm

60 — Weight of the load

Sometimes two levers of the first class are put together. These are called double levers.

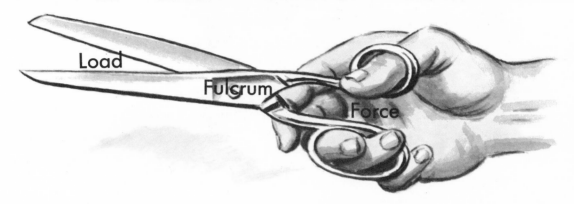

This pair of scissors is a double lever.

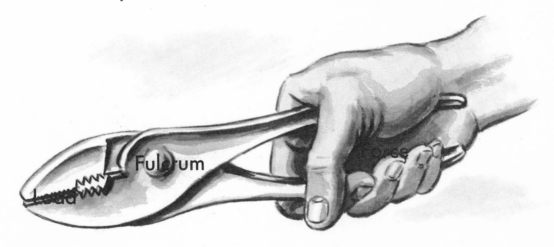

A pair of pliers is also a double lever of the first class.

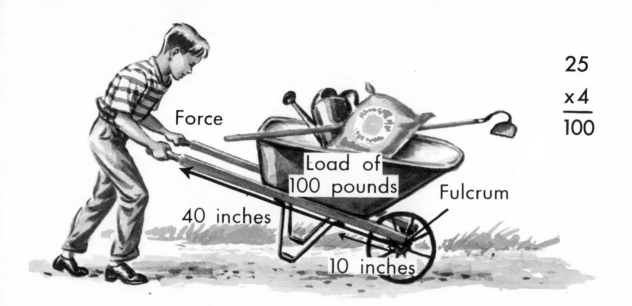

25
x4
___
100

Second-class Levers

In the levers of the second class, the load is always between the force and the fulcrum.

The wheelbarrow is a second-class lever.

The distance from the force to the fulcrum is 4 times greater than the distance from the fulcrum to the load. The amount of lift or force the boy gives to the handles is multiplied 4 times as it travels along to the load. So a force of 25 pounds is all that is needed to lift this 100-pound load.

Third-class Levers

Levers of the third class always have the force between the fulcrum and the load. Levers of this class do not multiply force. But they do help man move objects faster and greater distances than he could without them.

The girl's hand moves from point A to point B as she sweeps. The bottom of the broom moves much farther than the girl's hand. The bottom of the broom also moves faster than the girl's hand.

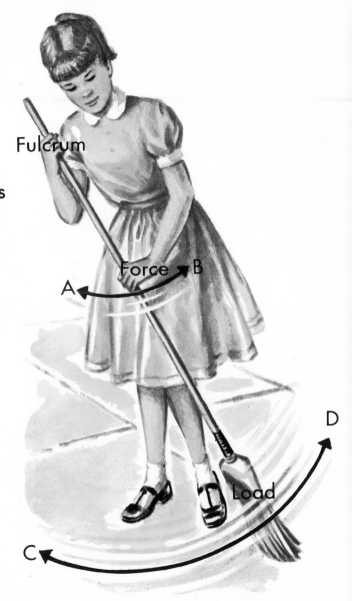

Fulcrum

A — Force → B

C ← → D

Load

The pictures on this page show more examples of third-class levers.

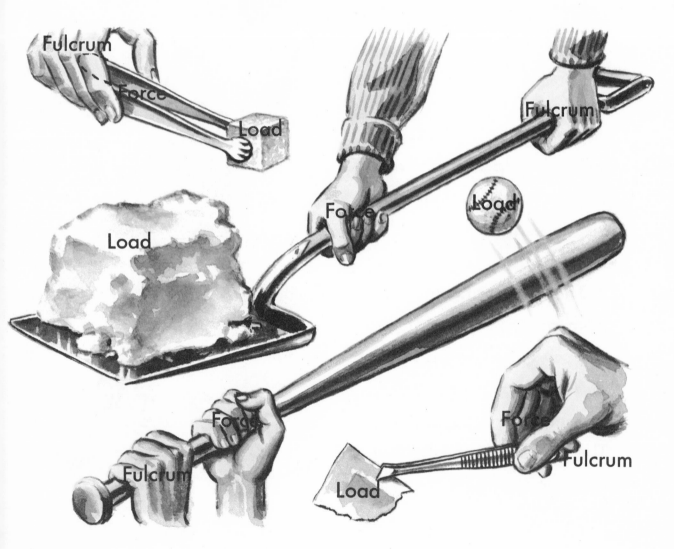

THE PULLEY

A pulley is a wheel with a groove in its rim. A rope fits into the groove of the wheel. As the rope is drawn, the wheel turns.

The picture shows a single fixed pulley. "Single" means one, and "fixed" means staying in one place. See how the frame holds the pulley wheel to the board. The wheel can turn, but it stays in one place.

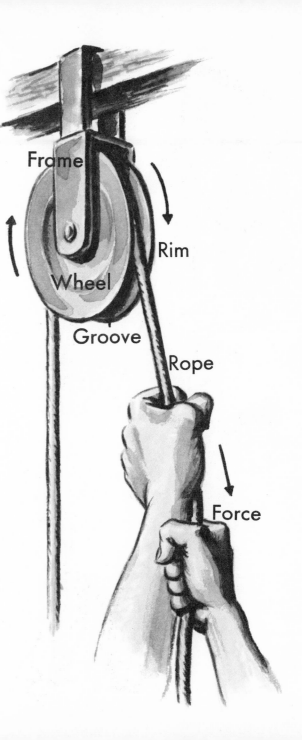

Frame

Rim

Wheel

Groove

Rope

Force

This man is using a single fixed pulley to lift the hay into the barn.

The hay or the load weighs 20 pounds. Using this pulley, the man must pull with 20 pounds of force in order to lift the hay.

A single fixed pulley such as this does not multiply the force. But it is easier for the man to lift the hay with the pulley than it would be for him to carry the hay. The man can stay in one place. He can use the weight of his body to pull down as he lifts the load up.

This picture shows a kind of pulley that does multiply the force. A pulley that multiplies force must have a movable wheel and a fixed wheel.

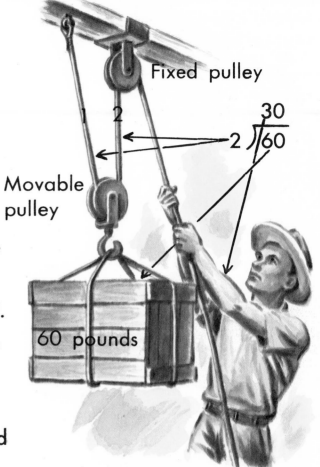

Fixed pulley

Movable pulley

60 pounds

$$\begin{array}{r} 30 \\ 2\,\overline{\smash{)}60} \end{array}$$

See the fixed pulley at the top. See the movable pulley to which the load is fastened. The movable pulley moves in the same direction as the load moves.

This kind of pulley is called a block and tackle.

To find how much force is needed to lift the box weighing 60 pounds, we count the strands of ropes coming from the movable wheel. There are 2.

Now we divide the weight of the load by 2.

A force of 30 pounds will lift the 60-pound box.

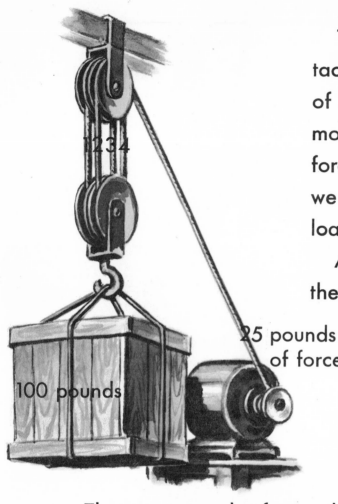

This is a double block and tackle. There are four strands of rope coming from the movable wheel. To find the force needed to lift the box, we divide the weight of the load by 4.

A pull of 25 pounds lifts the box.

25 pounds of force

100 pounds

1234

$$4\overline{)100}^{25}$$

The more strands of rope there are in the pulley, the easier it is to lift the load.

But more rope in the pulley also means that the force has to pull longer. For example, to lift this load 1 foot, the motor must wind 4 feet of rope.

THE INCLINED PLANE

An inclined plane is any surface slanted at an angle.
"Inclined" means slanted, and "plane" means surface.
Both children are riding up inclined planes.

Force of
20 pounds

4 feet

Load of
20 pounds

The boy wants to lift this wagon onto the platform. The platform is 4 feet high. The wagon weighs 20 pounds.

If the boy pulls the wagon straight up, he must pull with a force equal to the weight of the wagon.

He uses 20 pounds of force to lift the wagon onto the platform.

This time the boy uses a board which is 8 feet long. He puts the board at an angle to the platform. The board is an inclined plane.

A force of about 10 pounds now pulls the wagon up the inclined plane.

It is easier to pull the wagon up the inclined plane than to lift it straight up onto the platform.

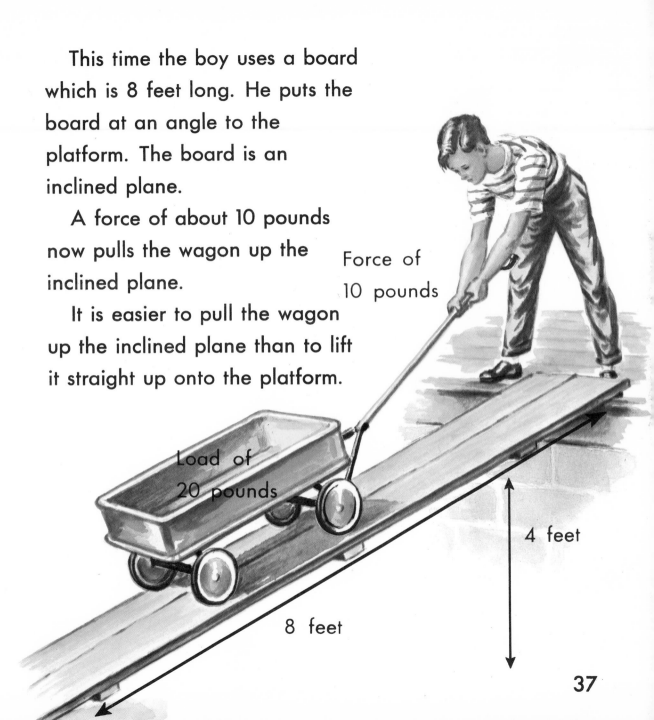

Force of
10 pounds

Load of
20 pounds

4 feet

8 feet

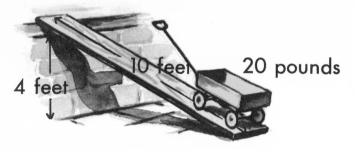

This is the way to find the force needed to move an object up an inclined plane.

Multiply the height of the platform in feet by the weight of the object in pounds.

$$20$$
$$\times 4$$
$$\overline{80}$$

Divide the answer by the length of the inclined plane measured in feet.

$$10\overline{)80}^{8}$$

A force of 8 pounds will pull the wagon onto the platform.

If the inclined plane is 20 feet long, a force of only 4 pounds will be needed to pull the wagon. The longer the inclined plane is, the less force will be needed to move the wagon.

$$20$$
$$\times 4$$
$$\overline{80}$$

$$20\overline{)80}^{4}$$

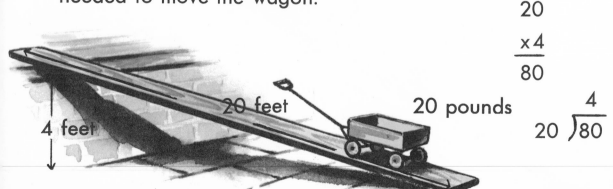

THE WEDGE AND THE SCREW

A wedge is two inclined planes joined together like this:

See the two inclined planes joined together. See the sharp point.

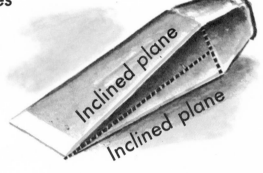

We push the wedge through things.

In goes the wedge. The wood splits apart.

We use wedges every day. All of these tools
are wedges. See the sharp points.

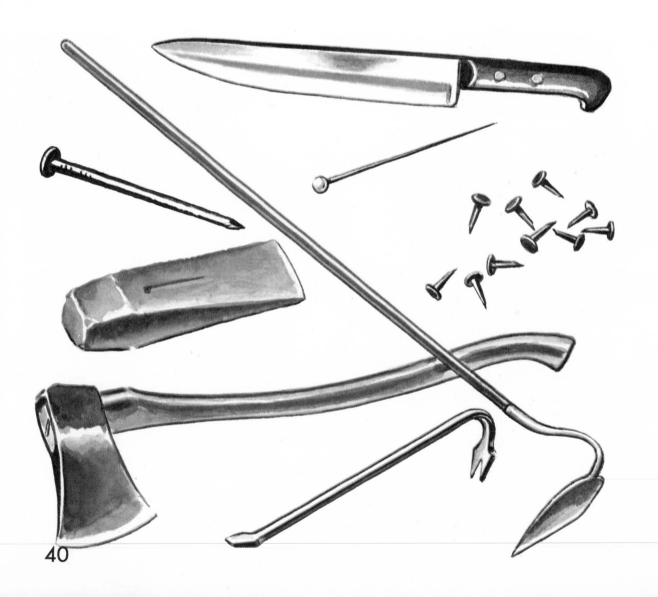

A screw is a kind of
inclined plane, too. A thin
ribbon of metal winds up
and around another piece
of metal. This ribbon can
be thought of as an
inclined plane.

We can see how the metal ribbon winds around
a metal rod in a screw by wrapping a piece of paper
cut like an inclined plane around a pencil.

A screw can be used to
hold things together.
In the picture, the screw
is pushed tightly into wood.

Screws have many uses.

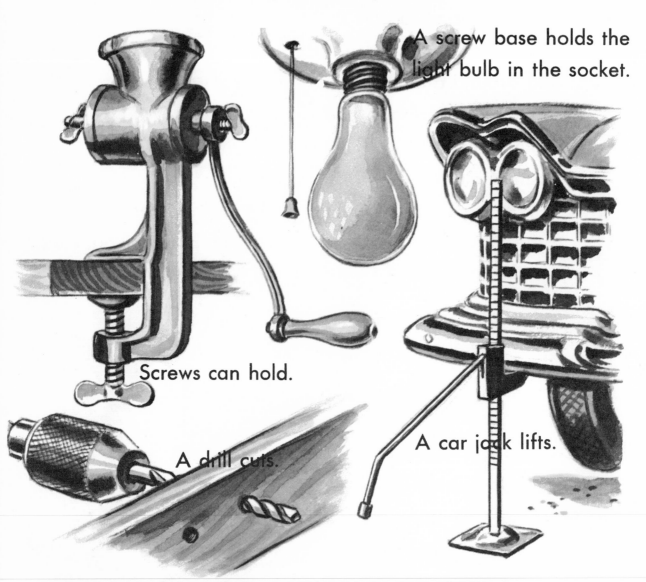

A screw base holds the light bulb in the socket.

Screws can hold.

A drill cuts.

A car jack lifts.

Wedge

Lever

Wheel and axle

BIG MACHINES

Big machines are made up
of two or more simple ones.
Here are some big
machines and some of the
simple machines in them.

Here is a wheel and axle. Turning the wheel turns the axle.

The rubber roller is around the axle.

Screws hold the sides of the typewriter together.

Pushing a key down pulls down on one end of the lever.

This makes the other end of the lever move to the paper. A letter on the end of the lever strikes the paper. The typewriter prints the letter.

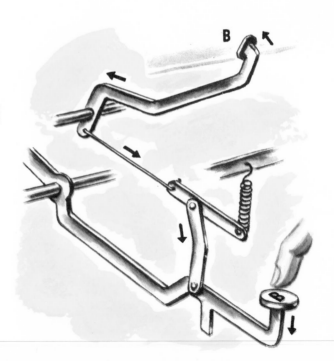

It is easy to open cans with this machine.

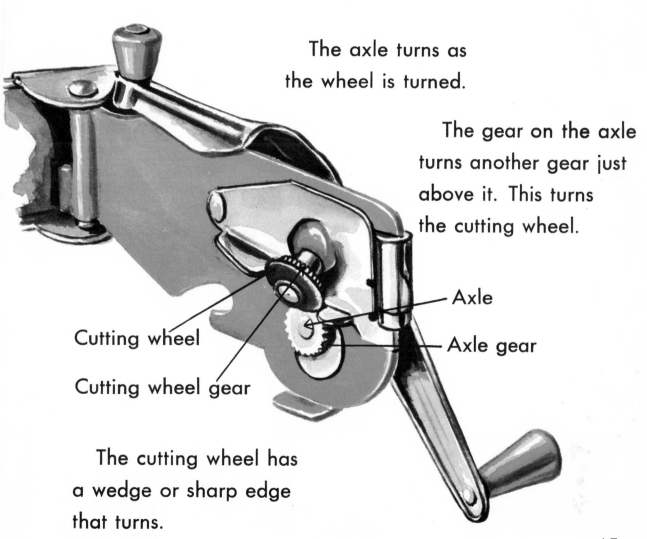

The axle turns as
the wheel is turned.

The gear on the axle
turns another gear just
above it. This turns
the cutting wheel.

Cutting wheel

Cutting wheel gear

Axle

Axle gear

The cutting wheel has
a wedge or sharp edge
that turns.

We use machines every day.
They make our work easier. Simple
machines do special things to make
our work easier. To use them wisely
we need to understand them.

A lever can be used to move things
with less force.

Wheels can be used to move things
more easily from place to place.
Big wheels can make small wheels
turn fast.

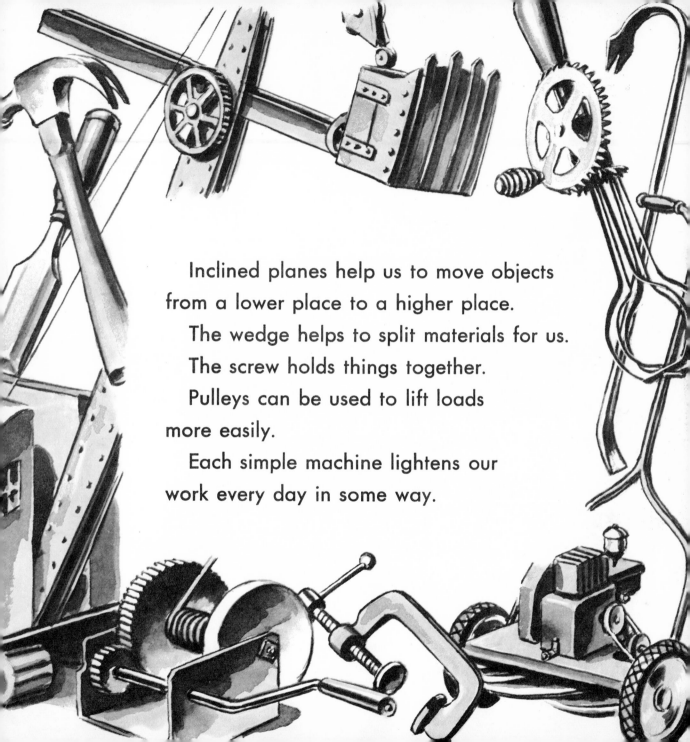

Inclined planes help us to move objects from a lower place to a higher place.

The wedge helps to split materials for us.

The screw holds things together.

Pulleys can be used to lift loads more easily.

Each simple machine lightens our work every day in some way.

PICTURE DICTIONARY

FIXED PULLEY A pulley which is fastened to a steady object. The rope spins around the wheel, but the wheel always stays in the same place. 32

FORCE Something which moves an object. This motor is the force which makes the wheels turn. 13

FRICTION The rubbing or scraping together of two objects. Friction works against or tries to stop motion. The blade, held tightly against the moving wheel, slows the speed of the wheel and tends to stop its spinning. 13

FULCRUM The support or steady object on which a lever rests. These children are using a log as a fulcrum for their seesaw. 20

LOAD Anything that is to be moved. 21

MOVABLE PULLEY A pulley which is not fastened to a steady object. The wheel can spin at different places along the rope. 33